ZENDAYA
Making a Difference as a Movie and TV Star

By Katie Kawa

KidHaven
PUBLISHING

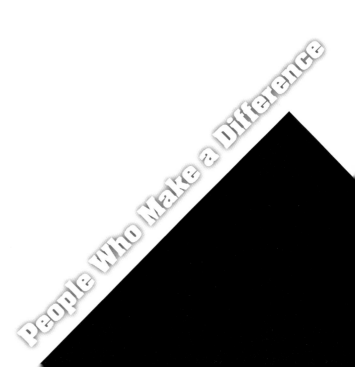

People Who Make a Difference

Published in 2025 by
KidHaven Publishing, an Imprint of Greenhaven Publishing, LLC
2544 Clinton St.
Buffalo, NY 14224

Designer: Deanna Lepovich
Editor: Katie Kawa

Photo credits: Cover, p. 9 Tinseltown/Shutterstock.com; pp. 5, 11 DFree/Shutterstock.com; p. 7 Sky Cinema/Shutterstock.com; p. 13 Sipa USA/Alamy Stock Photo; p. 15 AFF/Alamy Stock Photo; p. 17 FashionStock.com/Shutterstock.com; pp. 19, 20 Kathy Hutchins/Shutterstock.com; p. 21 T.Sumaetho/Shutterstock.com.

Library of Congress Cataloging-in-Publication Data

Names: Kawa, Katie, author.
Title: Zendaya : making a difference as a movie and TV star / Katie Kawa.
Description: Buffalo, New York : KidHaven Publishing, 2025. | Series:
    People who make a difference | Includes index.
Identifiers: LCCN 2024010816 | ISBN 9781534548138 (library binding) | ISBN
    9781534548121 (paperback) | ISBN 9781534548145 (ebook)
Subjects: LCSH: Zendaya, 1996–Juvenile literature. | Actors–United
    States–Biography–Juvenile literature. | Singers–United
    States–Biography–Juvenile literature. | Models (Persons)–United
    States–Biography–Juvenile literature. | LCGFT: Biographies.
Classification: LCC PN2287.Z47 K39 2025 | DDC 791.4302/8092
    [B]–dc23/eng/20230313
LC record available at https://lccn.loc.gov/2024010816

Printed in the United States of America

Some of the images in this book illustrate individuals who are models. The depictions do not imply actual situations or events.

CPSIA compliance information: Batch #CSKH25: For further information contact Greenhaven Publishing LLC at 1-844-317-7404.

Please visit our website, www.greenhavenpublishing.com. For a free color catalog of all our high-quality books, call toll free 1-844-317-7404 or fax 1-844-317-7405.

Find us on

CONTENTS

IN THE SPOTLIGHT

Zendaya Maree Stoermer Coleman is so famous the world knows her simply by her first name. There's no one else like Zendaya! From her bold fashion choices to her roles, or parts, in popular movies and TV shows, she knows how to stand out.

Zendaya knows the spotlight is always on her, and she uses that to bring others into the spotlight with her. She creates opportunities for Black voices to be heard on **social media**, in the world of fashion, and in Hollywood. By using her **platform** to lift others up and tell new and important stories, Zendaya is making a difference!

In Her Words

"I'm an actress, but I'm also just a person who has a heart and wants to do the right thing."

— Interview with Black Lives Matter (BLM) co-founder Patrisse Cullors for *InStyle* magazine from August 2020

Zendaya has a lot of power in the worlds of fashion, movies, and TV. She's using that power for good!

A BORN PERFORMER

Zendaya has been **performing** since she was a little kid. She was born on September 1, 1996, in Oakland, California. Her parents worked as teachers, and they supported her love of dancing, singing, and acting.

Zendaya began dancing at an early age, and she also acted in plays at the California Shakespeare Theater. Performing the works of the famous writer William Shakespeare helped Zendaya prepare for her future as an actress. Zendaya also studied acting at different theater **programs** in California and at the Oakland School for the Arts. She kept dancing, too, and danced in music videos and **commercials**.

In Her Words

"I think my parents [**instilled**] in me at a very young age [the ability] to stick up for myself. If you don't like something, you say it. If something makes you uncomfortable, you tell somebody."

— Interview with *InStyle* magazine from October 2021

Some of Zendaya's first jobs were modeling clothes for stores such as Macy's and Old Navy. Today, she's a fashion icon—someone who's known around the world for her style.

DISNEY CHANNEL STAR

Zendaya was looking for her chance to step into the spotlight, and she found it on the Disney Channel. In 2010, she began playing the part of Rocky Blue on the Disney Channel TV show *Shake It Up*. She continued to play Rocky until 2013. That year, she came in second place on the TV show *Dancing with the Stars*.

Zendaya also starred in the Disney Channel movies *Frenemies*, which came out in 2012, and *Zapped*, which came out in 2014. She got her next starring role in the Disney Channel show *K.C. Undercover*, which was on TV from 2015 to 2018.

In Her Words

"Always try to **focus** on creating and doing things that genuinely [truly] make you happy, things that feel good in your gut and your heart, and you really can't go wrong."

— Interview with *Harper's Bazaar* magazine from February 2022

While Zendaya was becoming a Disney Channel star, she was also making music! In 2011, she released, or put out, her first song, "Swag It Out." In 2013, she released her first album, *Zendaya*.

9

SUCCESS WITH SPIDER-MAN

Zendaya made the leap from TV to the big screen in July 2017, when she played the part of Michelle (better known as MJ) in the movie *Spider-Man: Homecoming*. There had been other Spider-Man movies before with other MJs, but Zendaya was the first Black woman to play Spider-Man's girlfriend.

The movie was a hit, and people were excited to see how Zendaya brought MJ to life. She played the character again in 2019 in *Spider-Man: Far From Home* and in 2021 in *Spider-Man: No Way Home*. That movie made more money than any other movie in 2021!

In Her Words

"Just because you haven't done something before doesn't mean it can't be done."

— Interview with *InStyle* magazine from October 2021

Zendaya met Tom Holland, who plays Spider-Man (also known as Peter Parker), while working on *Spider-Man: Homecoming*.

AN AWARD-WINNING ACTRESS

Zendaya played big parts in other movies too. She played Anne Wheeler in *The Greatest Showman*, which came out in December 2017. In 2021, she acted in a **drama** for adults called *Malcolm & Marie* and a **science fiction** movie called *Dune*. Zendaya's voice has also been used in **animated** movies, including *Smallfoot* in 2018 and *Space Jam: A New Legacy* in 2021.

In 2019, Zendaya returned to TV in the role of Rue Bennett on *Euphoria*. Zendaya won an Emmy Award—the highest honor given in the TV business—in 2020 for playing Rue. She won another Emmy for this role in 2022.

Zendaya is shown here after winning her second Emmy Award. When she won her first Emmy Award in 2020, she became the youngest woman to win the award for Outstanding Lead Actress in a Drama Series.

In Her Words

"We learn how to be a person not just through interactions [dealing with people], but by watching movies and TV. You want to be like your favorite character."

— Interview with actor Colman Domingo for *Interview* magazine from December 2021

MAKING A STYLE STATEMENT

As a successful actress, Zendaya is often seen at important events. In 2015, she was seen at the Oscars—the most important event in the movie business. She wore her hair in dreadlocks—a hairstyle mostly worn by people of color that's made up of ropelike strands of hair.

When a reporter seemed to make fun of Zendaya's hair, Zendaya posted on social media about how it's wrong to judge people by their looks. She wore her hair in dreadlocks to show the beauty of Black hair, and she's continued to use her platform to **celebrate** Black points of view in beauty and fashion.

Zendaya is shown here at the 2015 Oscars. Ever since this moment, she's become known for using her style to make a statement. For example, when she appeared on the cover of *InStyle* magazine in 2020, she only wore things by Black designers—people who create clothes.

In Her Words

"My wearing my hair in locs [dreadlocks] on an Oscar red carpet was to showcase them in a positive light, to remind people of color that our hair is good enough. To me locs are a symbol [sign] of strength and beauty, almost like a lion's mane."

— Instagram post from February 2015

RAISING MONEY AND AWARENESS

Zendaya has used her fame to shine a spotlight on Black voices in the fashion world. She's also used her fame to shine a spotlight on other things she cares about.

Zendaya has often used her birthday to help raise money for causes close to her heart. For her 18th birthday, Zendaya asked her fans to give money to help feed hungry children. Her 19th birthday became a chance to raise money for three boys she met in Africa whose parents had died. On her 21st birthday, she raised money to help people after Hurricane Harvey—a big storm that hit Texas in 2017.

In Her Words

"More than anything, I just want to tell people that your voice does matter. The little things do matter."

— Interview with Black Lives Matter (BLM) co-founder Patrisse Cullors for *InStyle* magazine from August 2020

Zendaya has even modeled dresses for a cause! She's shown here in 2015 at the Go Red for Women Red Dress Collection event in New York City. This event raises awareness of efforts to fight heart problems in women.

IMPORTANT ISSUES

Zendaya has said there are people who know more than she does about important issues, and she wants to put them in the spotlight. For example, Zendaya cares a lot about the Black Lives Matter (BLM) movement. This is a movement that calls attention to the problems of **racism** and **violence** against Black people. In 2020, she allowed BLM co-founder Patrisse Cullors to take over her Instagram so her followers could learn more about BLM from someone at the center of it.

Women's issues are also important to Zendaya. She attended the Women's March on Washington in 2017 to stand up for women's rights.

In Her Words

"If I don't know something, then I ask people who are actually on the front lines doing the work. I'm up in the bleachers [stands], not on the field. So I always think, 'How can I cheer you on and be a part of something greater than myself?'"

— Interview with Black Lives Matter (BLM) co-founder Patrisse Cullors for *InStyle* magazine from August 2020

The Life of Zendaya

1996
Zendaya Maree Stoermer Coleman is born on September 1 in Oakland, California.

2010
Zendaya begins playing Rocky Blue on *Shake It Up*.

2012
Zendaya acts in the Disney Channel movie *Frenemies*.

2013
Shake It Up ends, Zendaya comes in second place on *Dancing with the Stars*, and the album *Zendaya* is released.

2014
Zendaya stars in the Disney Channel movie *Zapped*.

2015–2018
Zendaya stars in the TV show *K.C. Undercover*.

2017
Zendaya plays MJ in *Spider-Man: Homecoming* and plays Anne Wheeler in *The Greatest Showman*.

2018
Zendaya voices the character of Meechee in *Smallfoot*.

2019
Zendaya begins starring in the TV show *Euphoria* and plays MJ again in *Spider-Man: Far From Home*.

2020
Zendaya shows her support for BLM by having one of its co-founders take over her Instagram, and she wins an Emmy Award for *Euphoria*.

2021
Zendaya is part of four movies: *Malcolm & Marie*, *Space Jam: A New Legacy*, *Dune*, and *Spider-Man: No Way Home*.

2022
Zendaya wins her second Emmy Award for *Euphoria*.

2024
Zendaya acts in the movies *Dune: Part Two* and *Challengers*.

Zendaya has played many different characters during her time as a movie and TV star. She's said she hopes she can make a difference through those characters. She wants to play parts that help people feel seen and help people understand those who are different from them.

19

TRUE TO HERSELF

Zendaya isn't afraid to tell the truth. In 2015, she called out a magazine that changed a picture of her to make her look different and posted the real picture on Instagram. She wanted to remind women to love themselves as they are.

Love is important to Zendaya. She loves her work, including the movies *Dune: Part Two* and *Challengers*, which came out in 2024. She loves her fans. She also loves helping others by using her style, her roles, and her voice to tell important stories. Zendaya has found fame while staying true to herself, and that's helped her make a difference!

20

In Her Words

"Hopefully my ability to be a storyteller, to make those stories that I haven't seen, to showcase different forms of Black love and the different colors of our emotional experience [feelings]—that will be my speaking out. That's my action."

— Interview with actor Colman Domingo for *Interview* magazine from December 2021

Be Like Zendaya!

Learn more about the Black Lives Matter movement and what you can do to fight racism.

Be kind to your body, and don't compare how you look to pictures on social media or in magazines. Remind your friends and family of this too!

Learn more about causes you care about. One way to do that is by talking to people who know a lot about an issue and asking them questions.

Ask a trusted adult to take you to a march or another event for a cause you care about.

Wear clothes and hairstyles that help you feel confident, or sure of yourself. Help your friends find what makes them feel confident too!

For your birthday, ask for people to give money to a good cause instead of buying you presents.

If you use social media, use it in a positive way. Share things about important issues, and only share posts and pictures you know are real and true.

If you see someone being bullied for how they look, tell a trusted adult, and help the person being bullied feel better.

Zendaya knows that the best way to make a difference is by being yourself and standing up for what you love and what you know is right. These are some ways you can follow her example!

GLOSSARY

animated: Made using a series of drawings, pictures, or computer-created images that are shown quickly one after another.

celebrate: To say that something is great or important.

commercial: A short clip shown on TV that is created to make people want to buy a good or service.

drama: A play, movie, or TV show that has many sad moments and often has a sad ending.

focus: To direct attention or effort at something.

instill: To cause to feel or have something slowly over time.

perform: To entertain people by singing, acting, or dancing.

platform: An opportunity to talk publicly.

program: A set of classes or events related to a certain subject.

racism: The practice of treating others poorly because they are part of a different race, or group of people who look alike in certain ways. This word also relates to governments and societies that allow one race to be treated better than others.

science fiction: A kind of story that is not real and that deals with the effects of real or pretend science on characters and their world.

social media: A collection of websites and applications, or apps, that allow users to interact with each other and create online communities.

violence: The use of bodily force to hurt others.

FOR MORE INFORMATION

WEBSITES

About: Convoy of Hope

convoyofhope.org/about

One group Zendaya has worked closely with is Convoy of Hope, and this part of its website tells visitors about the work it does to help people and how it got started.

IMDb: Zendaya

www.imdb.com/name/nm3918035

Zendaya's page on the Internet Movie Database has a list of her movies and TV shows, as well as facts about her life.

BOOKS

Anderson, Kirsten. *Who Is Zendaya?* New York, NY: Penguin Workshop, 2022.

Andrews, Elizabeth. *Zendaya: Emmy-Winning Entertainer*. Minneapolis, MN: Pop!, 2024.

Shea, Therese. *Zendaya*. Buffalo, NY: PowerKids Press, 2022.

INDEX